# THE DIVERSITY OF SKINKS

The beginning terrarium hobbyist interested in lizards often tends to look only at the common, colorful, easy to find species such as Green Anoles and Green Iguanas. But there is no reason to look at only these familiar pet lizards for either the first lizard pet or a more expensive special pet. The more adventurous hobbyist could always try a skink.

You've all seen skinks in the pet shop though you might not have paid too much attention to them. The typical skinks are tube-like lizards usually with tails about as

often with comb-like scales at one edge to help prevent the entry of sand and soil during burrowing. Most species are glossy brownish to tan, often with dark crossbars over the back or, even more commonly, dark stripes along the upper sides; red on the head and sides is common, as is a blue tint to the tail. Though the teeth are not obvious, the bigger species of skinks can have a painful nip, though they rarely draw blood.

With very few exceptions, skinks are burrowers, hiders under logs and leaf litter, or

R. D. BARTLETT

A typical skink: *Mabuya brevicollis* of dry eastern Africa. This is a male, as told by its reddish sides.

long as the body and four rather short legs with long toes. The scales are very regular in shape on the body and head, rather large, shiny, and in distinct rows both above and below. Often the snout is tapering and the head appears somewhat flattened. There usually is a distinct "ear hole" on each side of the head,

dwellers in dry prairies and even deserts. The typical skink uses the tapered snout, flattened body, and glossy scales to aid in burrowing, the legs often being held to the sides and the lizard moving by wriggling like a short snake. Many burrowing skinks have very small legs or have lost the legs and are even more snake-like than the common species. In some skinks the eyelids have fused over the eye (for added protection to the eye during burrowing) and a transparent window has developed in the eyelids to allow the lizards to sense light and movement. Most larger skinks, however, have normal, movable eyelids and blink, so they lack the snaky-stare of lizards with fused eyelids.

At least a few species of skinks

more uniform the further you go south into the American tropics, with only a few species in South America. A few typically African and eastern Asian species reach into Europe, while the southern Asian skinks are relatively poorly known and generally dully colored, though some represent potentially beautiful or even stunning lizards that eventually might enter the terrarium hobby. Australia is literally loaded with

R. D. BARTLETT

The Australian *Egernia kingi*, a nearly smooth "spiny-tailed" skink from Australia.

are found on every continent (except Antarctica, as might be expected), though there is a greater diversity of genera and species in Africa and Australia than perhaps anywhere else. Though North America has quite a few species, skinks are fewer and

skinks, from tiny and almost worm-like species to the gigantic blue-tongues, but currently Australian laws virtually prohibit export or even keeping in their native country of most Australian animals. Presently most of the skinks you'll find in the pet shops come from North America (a few common *Eumeces* species), Africa (another *Eumeces* or two, plus *Scincus, Chalcides, Lygosoma [Riopa],* and several *Mabuya* species), various Asian points (*Lamprolepis [=Dasia], Tropidophorus, Corucia,* plus more *Mabuya* species), and New Guinea plus Australia, known as Australasia (*Egernia* and *Tiliqua,* considered by many to be the

herpetologists who are working on the family have been setting up many small genera for species that once were put in a few really big genera, but most of these new genera are based on minute characters of the skeleton that the average hobbyist is unlikely to be able to check. One genus even is based on the presence or absence of tubercles on the eggshell!

This is not to say that the

G. DINGERKUS

*Acontias* is a heavy-bodied southern African skink that has lost typical external legs, as have several other skinks.

ultimate skinks). Don't worry too much about these names now, because we'll go through all of them again later in separate chapters on each continent, the only natural way to consider the diversity of skinks.

Skinks belong to the family Scincidae, a totally confusing group of lizards that are poorly understood by scientists. There is no agreement on the number of genera and species, but usual estimates indicate about 85 genera and over 900 species, with other estimates to over 1000 species. Lately the several

names used by specialists are unnecessary, but hobbyists should not worry too much about identification to species in this group of lizards and often shouldn't even spend too much time trying to figure out the genus. Most skinks are very similar in their requirements for successful terrarium maintenance, and it sometimes is possible to guess the habitat requirements of a "mystery" species by just looking at its general structure and comparing it to a few common types. Probably fewer than 50 skink species enter the hobby on a regular basis, and many of even this small number are virtually impossible to identify to species. Even the wholesalers have identification problems, so this is one of those lizard groups where each visit to the pet shop could lead to a fascinating new challenge for the more advanced keeper, and at a reasonable price.

Skinks are among the few inexpensive lizards that make good pets. Four or five common and very good pet species are affordable to even the beginner, and they also require only simple and inexpensive terraria. The species in this book tend to live at least five or six years, with some reaching ages of ten or even 15 years. They are adaptable, have wide temperature tolerances, don't need special misting machines and the like, and eat almost any insect food that will fit into their jaws. Other species are among the most expensive of the lizards but still are not hard to keep under a bit more specialized care. The largest and most unusual skinks, such as the blue-tongues and Monkey Skink, are readily available as captive-bred stock, though you might have to pay a week's or a month's salary for a pair. The cheapest species usually are, unfortunately, wild-caught though many could be bred in captivity with more attention to proper feeding and over-wintering routines.

We'll try to talk about a broad range of skinks in this book, from the most expensive and bizarre to true beginner's species not much more expensive than that short-lived Green Anole, and even easier to keep. I'll try to give you the basic care and feeding instructions you will need for any skink you are likely to run across in the pet shop or on a dealer's

The rarest of the rare: an albino Eastern Blue-tongued Skink, *Tiliqua scincoides.*

K. H. SWITAK

R. D. BARTLETT

The depressed snout of *Scincus scincus*, the Sandfish, helps it swim through loose sand.

list. I'll even try to give you the basics of breeding routines for some of the species, though admittedly except for the largest (and most expensive) species most skinks are not simple to breed in captivity.

Skinks are simple lizards. They are simple in structure (no elaborate crests or horns or strange scales), simple to keep and feed, and simple to get hooked on. I think that if you try a good skink you'll find them a step beyond most other lizards and a neglected group that provides much satisfaction for every level hobbyist.

*Chalcides chalcides* is an African desert skink that has reduced the legs to tiny useless flaps.

D. GREEN

J.MERLI

Portrait of a Monkey Skink, *Corucia zebrata*, perhaps the most unusual skink of them all.

# DIVERSE HABITATS

Though "a skink is a skink" may be true as a general observation, that doesn't mean they all need the same type of care. Because of differences in adult size (commonly from less than 6 inches to over 24 inches), natural habitat (desert to rainforest), and temperature requirements (cool temperate to hot desert) within the familiar pet species, at least three different types of enclosures are best to cover the needs of the family. I'll discuss each type in general terms here, but remember to look at the species discussions for more details.

## TEMPERATE LITTER CAGES

The most common and inexpensive skinks are various species of *Mabuya* and *Eumeces* from Asia, Africa, and North America, the five-lined skinks and rainbow skinks. Though there are differences in requirements for the various species, to most keepers these skinks are essentially similar in appearance, size, and cage needs.

Because most of these skinks run from about 8 inches to 12 inches or so in adult length, they can be kept in a standard all-glass terrarium or a standard sliding-door reptile cage. In a pinch a terrarium of just 10-gallon capacity (40 liters) will do for a couple of skinks, but be generous and give them at least 20 gallons (80 liters) so they can be more active and less likely to fight. Though skinks are not excessively territorial, males in breeding condition (usually recognizable by heavy jowls and some red on the head or sides) can be touchy, and if three or more young skinks are kept in one cage they definitely will fight over food. The more room, the better. Tall terraria are not necessary for this type of skink.

Five-lines and rainbows are not especially good climbers, but be sure to provide a secure, ventilated top for the cage. If a skink can follow a branch to an upper corner of the cage, it probably will take the last step and go over the top. A screened lid also helps you maintain adequate ventilation by covering half with a sheet of plastic and leaving half open to air circulation.

Skinks are burrowers, and this must be reflected in their substrate and hiding places. Provide a base layer of at least 2 inches of common bark mulch or a hardwood bedding material such as aspen or cypress mulch. Orchid bark mix, sand, and potting soil are good as mixtures with the basic mulch substrate. Avoid pine and cedar shavings as they are very resinous and may be distasteful to skinks; some keepers even believe they will kill small lizards. Cover the basic substrate with leaf litter, pine needles, living moss, long-strand sphagnum moss, and similar loose materials that allow the substrate to breathe, letting excess moisture evaporate yet never drying completely. You'll be misting the cage once or twice a week to maintain humidity levels, but these lizards are not especially sensitive to drier air, though they like humidity levels of about 60% or so most of the time.

Hiding places are a must with skinks. Try to give each specimen at least two different places to hide, more if you are keeping young lizards. Pieces of cork bark, broken flowerpot pieces, and ceramic hideboxes all work well. Try placing at least some of the hiding places partially into the substrate so the skink can burrow from one hiding place to another without coming into sight if it feels stressed. Though these skinks are not especially shy and will be almost as active during the day as at night once they adapt, for the first few weeks after you get them from the pet shop they will hide and try to get the feel of the terrarium. Don't stress

them more by forcing them into the light when they don't want to be seen. A few sturdy branches that are well-anchored will serve as activity and basking sites for some skinks, especially if they run from within the substrate and are only a few inches above the ground. African *Mabuya* especially like to climb and bask on groups of rocks. Living plants are unnecessary in skink cages and probably will be demolished. Keep it simple and you will be better off.

A shallow water bowl should be provided because most skinks drink as well as lick water from leaves and branches. Change the water each day. If you notice aggressive behavior around the water bowl, provide two

PHOTO COURTESY OF RIVER TANK

A paludarium (above) may not be the most appropriate skink habitat, but many humid forest species, such as the New Caledonian *Lioscincus steindachneri* shown below, will take to water to escape predators and swim fairly well.

G. DINGERKUS

bowls in the tank. A few bits of gravel or broken crockery will prevent accidental drowning in the bowl. Many skinks in this group are good swimmers, but few will bathe in the water bowl.

Heating for the North American species is not really important during most of the year, as they will do well at typical home temperature levels (about 72°F, 22°C). African and Indonesian rainbow skinks like it a bit

some individuals probably never bask or do so only when the mood hits them.

Whether special lighting is necessary for typical skinks is a matter of debate among keepers. Most do bask, but they typically are most active and feed mostly at night. Additionally, the heavy and reflective scales will bounce back most ultraviolet light. Perhaps a compromise is best by providing a simple white fluorescent bulb and

PHOTO COURTESY OF HAGEN

Small plastic terraria can be used to house small skinks and baby skinks and as temporary quarters for larger skinks while their regular quarters are being cleaned.

warmer, about 75°F (24°C). All will tolerate temperatures to 80°F (27°C) with no problems. A temperature gradient should be established in the substrate by providing a small heating pad at one corner of the tank, allowing the opposite corner to remain cool. Undertank heating pads and heat tapes work satisfactorily, as will a hot rock of moderate size in one corner. Many of these skinks will bask, so it doesn't hurt to provide a flat basking rock with a basking light in the corner with the heater. These are not especially "hot" baskers, and

a broad-spectrum reptile bulb in a double holder. Special UV lights would seem to be unnecessary. Short light cycles of only eight to ten hours a day, reduced to five or six hours during the cool months, seem to work well, though many keepers prefer a 12-hour day. The heater can be operated on the same cycle so only one timer is necessary.

Small individuals of five-lined and rainbow skinks can be maintained in roomy plastic sweater boxes as well as *TropiQuariums*. These can be set up much like true terraria, just

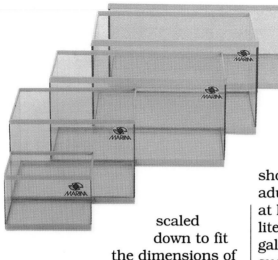

All-glass tanks remain the most simple type of terrarium and the easiest to obtain. Almost any skink can be housed correctly in an aquarium if given the proper substrate. Photo courtesy Hagen.

Australian *Egernia* species.

The size of the terrarium should be somewhat related to the adult size of the skink, but allow at least a 10-gallon terrarium (40 liters) for the small species and 20 gallons (80 liters) for large species such as the Berber Skink. Start with a deep (3 inches) layer of fine sand as a substrate. Because many of these species burrow in sand (especially *Chalcides* and *Scincus* species), it helps to keep part of the sand substrate slightly moist, the other part dry. A

scaled down to fit the dimensions of the sweater box. A looser substrate works best in a sweater box and should be shallower than in a normal terrarium. The lid of the box should be correctly fitted with ventilation holes adequately screened to prevent escapes. Because these lizards do not climb a lot and are not especially light-sensitive, they are prime choices for maintaining in racks of boxes. Such racks can be homemade or purchased commercially and are excellent if you find you like skinks and want to keep many in a small space. They also are fine for breeding colonies and for raising small skinks. The only disadvantage is that they are difficult to show off to your friends, but you only need one display terrarium to fill this need.

### DESERT CAGES

Skinks from North Africa and the Middle East, including *Chalcides, Scincus,* and *Eumeces schneideri,* do best in a desert or semidesert terrarium, as do many

Terrarium carpeting provides an active lizard with sure footing during the food chase. If you feed your skink crickets in a separate small terrarium, be sure to put a lining on the bottom.

shallow partition across the bottom of the tank will help keep the moist (easier to burrow in) and dry areas separate. Top the sand with about 2 inches of a sand and pebble mix, kept loose. Calcium sand such as used in marine aquaria looks nice and provides some variety. Add an array of "tiny boulders," flat rocks, and cork bark hiding and basking places to finish off the cage. Plants are unnecessary and more of a nuisance than a help. Mist the cage daily, trying to keep the moist part moist and the dry part dry. Provide a shallow water bowl and remember to keep it fresh—water evaporates rapidly in a desert terrarium. (Water bowls may best be omitted in cages for *Scincus*.)

Keep the desert cage warmer than the temperate litter cage, about 85°F (30°C) during the day, dropping ten degrees or so at night. An appropriate undertank pad heater or heater tapes and cables will work well. Keep the dry area warmer than the moist area

A close-fitting, secure cover is necessary for any lizard terrarium.

(i.e., the heat gradient should run from hot and dry to a bit cooler and more moist). Additionally, most of these skinks like to bask and like heat. A hot rock mechanism and a flat rock with a basking light over it both work well, but one of each would be better in the larger cage. Basking areas should be allowed to reach about 100°F (38°C), but be sure a

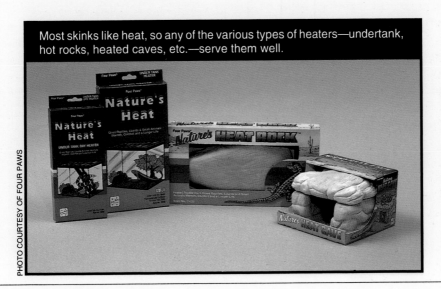

Most skinks like heat, so any of the various types of heaters—undertank, hot rocks, heated caves, etc.—serve them well.

Most skinks will demolish plants in their terrarium, so if you want a more natural look, use a good quality plastic plant from your pet shop.

of breeding, so the fluorescent overhead light fixture should contain an appropriate reptile bulb. Many of these skinks are day-active (diurnal), so provide a light and heat cycle of about 12 hours.

If kept in sweater boxes, be sure that your rack setup allows for a UV light source and, preferably, a safe basking area. In the privacy of a sweater box the substrate can be more shallow than in the terrarium if sufficient hiding places are provided and especially if the free end of the box is darkened.

### THE BIG GUYS

Blue-tongued skinks (*Tiliqua*) of various species are large animals that like to be kept in colonies, so here we face a space problem, because maintaining a group of stout 2-foot lizards can be tricky. (Also a "big guy" is the Monkey Skink or Solomons Giant Skink, but it requires rather different housing because of its climbing

cool relief area is available. Most keepers recommend ultraviolet light if desert skinks are to be kept healthy and have any chance

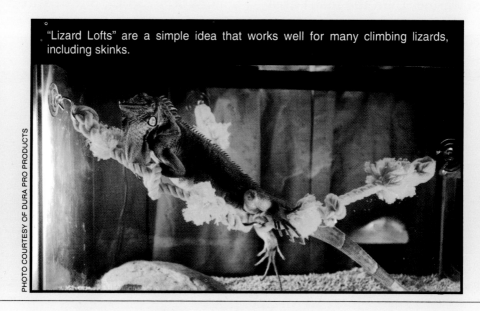

"Lizard Lofts" are a simple idea that works well for many climbing lizards, including skinks.

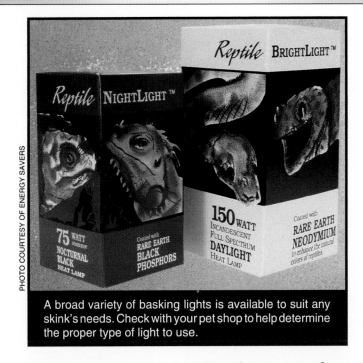

PHOTO COURTESY OF ENERGY SAVERS

A broad variety of basking lights is available to suit any skink's needs. Check with your pet shop to help determine the proper type of light to use.

lifestyle. I'll cover keeping this skink separately under the species discussion.) The smallest recommended size enclosure (often literally an enclosed part of a reptile room) is about 3 feet by 5 feet, the size of a large and expensive marine aquarium or an equally expensive commercial terrarium cage. Blue-tongues as a rule are dryland skinks, so they need a substrate of sand and gravel at least 3 or 4 inches deep. (The Pink-tongued Skink is a *Tiliqua* that likes a more moist habitat, so provide at least a part of its enclosure with a large area of potting soil and sphagnum moss that is sprayed daily; this actually might not be a bad idea with all these lizards.) After they adjust to captivity they do not burrow much, but they still need sufficient hideboxes to keep out of sight when they feel like it. Provide a good heat gradient.

Many keepers prefer putting a heating pad in the center of the terrarium and keeping the corners cool. You should maintain the temperature at about 85°F (30°C) or a bit more during the day, dropping by about ten degrees at night. A basking rock with an appropriate light and a large hot rock mechanism will provide for individual heat preferences. Most keepers like to have a source of UV light over the terrarium, though most blue-tongues are largely nocturnal in nature and probably get little UV under natural circumstances. Some species like to climb on low branches (of appropriate size and well-anchored), so the terrarium should be securely covered. A water bowl should be provided, as usual, and it is common practice to spray the lizards daily.

Blue-tongues often are kept in large plastic blanket boxes (babies

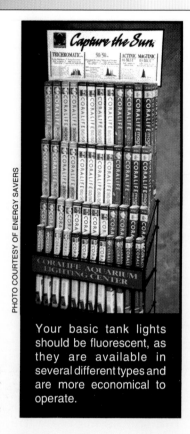

Your basic tank lights should be fluorescent, as they are available in several different types and are more economical to operate.

in sweater boxes) on racks, and they adapt well to these space-saving terraria. Just remember to provide a temperature gradient and lots of hiding places. In the sweater box environment small skinks often like paper towel cores and the like, including lengths of PVC pipe, as hiding places.

If you decide to keep blue-tongues, you have a problem that you do not face with other skinks: security from human invaders. These are popular, expensive animals, and there are numerous reports of the lizards being stolen during home burglaries and by visitors pocketing a specimen or two. A padlocked cover will prevent casual thefts, but there is no way to prevent losses to an actual thief. Home-owner insurance may not apply to captive reptile losses, and some companies in some areas have been known to refuse insurance to reptile-keepers. Many keepers suggest keeping a "low profile" if you have expensive reptiles today. This is an unfortunate situation, certainly, but something to remember.

The northern African *Chalcides sepsoides* would require a desert or other dry terrarium setup to prosper.

Skinks like to hide under logs and other objects on the ground, where they feed on the small insects so abundant there. This pile of logs would be an obvious place to search for skinks and a nice habitat to attempt to recreate.

*Egernia whiti* of Australia is a small, rather colorful but quite smooth "spiny-tailed" skink that is popular in the hobby.

# FEEDING

The vast majority of skinks are generalized insect feeders. They will take literally any insect in the right size range that they run across in the field. They also take snails and even slugs of the right size (especially the African and Australian skinks). This makes it easy to feed them, at least the larger species, because all you need is access to crickets, mealworms, and the occasional waxworm as the basic diet. You don't need to culture any of these animals as they usually are available from pet shops that cater to reptiles and from mailorder dealers advertising in fish and terrarium magazines. Keepers usually culture mealworms, however, and some like to culture crickets as well, so I'll include a few paragraphs on these animals later.

## FEEDING REGIMENS

Insects obviously provide the basic diet for most skinks, but even the common species like a bit of variety. The blue-tongues are unusual in being mostly vegetarians, feeding on fruit and greens in addition to insects, snails, and even pinkie mice, while Monkey Skinks are strict vegetarians. Additionally, most species will take some higher protein foods such as canned dog and cat food, and many like babyfoods of various types.

**Facing Page:** Coal Skinks, *Eumeces anthracinus*, are cool-adapted North American skinks that have proved hard to keep in captivity and are hard to feed. Most skinks, however, feed readily in the terrarium.

The best routine is to provide as much variety as possible. Most skinks are best fed at night after the lights go off. Feed every two days in most cases, about three or four times a week. There often is considerably aggression about the food bowl, so try to see which animals are feeding and which are being kept away. Missing toes and tears on the neck often are the result of food fights, especially among young skinks. If one skink, usually a dominant male either adult or juvenile, keeps the other skinks from the food bowl, provide several feeding areas, enough that the skinks don't have to associate.

Try to feed each species both insects and some fruit. Not all will accept fruit, but try it any way. Crickets are to be preferred as the main food insect because they are easy to gut-load with vitamins and calcium (see later) and have relatively little tough chitin compared to digestible matter in their bodies. Mealworms have more indigestible chitinous material and have been accused of causing gut impactions in some lizards, as well as being hard to kill by simply grabbing and chewing. Waxworms are very fatty and thus a good conditioning food, but they have a very tough cuticle that is hard to digest. Larger skinks will enjoy an occasional large grasshopper as well as some beetles (such as adult mealworms), while hatchling skinks need smaller insects. Provide some insects at each meal, perhaps making every other meal strictly crickets.

The alternate meal can consist

of both crickets and other insects along with a good brand of fruit babyfood (try several types) and perhaps some applesauce, of course with added vitamins and calcium. This is a good time to add a bit of canned cat or dog food to the meal, making the whole thing into a salad with a few pieces of diced apple, kiwi, or banana for variety. You'll find that some individuals of almost any species like fruit as much as insects, while others will take only the insects.

Blue-tongues, as we'll discuss later, like a basic meal of fruit salad with insects, snails, and even an occasional pinkie mouse added for variety. Most keepers tend to feed a fruit salad twice as often as an insect meal.

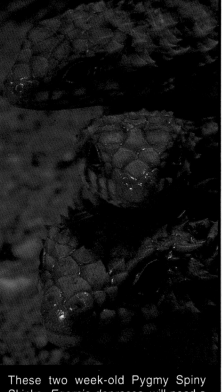

J. MERLI

These two week-old Pygmy Spiny Skinks, *Egernia depressa*, will need a varied diet fortified with calcium and vitamins to grow up like their mother.

Monkey Skinks like a mixture of fruits and greens such as spinach and dandelions, sometimes with a touch of fruit babyfood.

Water is essential to all skinks, and most need to drink from a bowl (Monkey Skinks may be an exception, preferring to lick droplets from leaves). The water must be kept fresh and must not be chlorinated or chemically contaminated. Tap water will work in most areas if it is allowed to air for at least a day before being offered. Water used for misting (mist the cage and fixtures but not the lizards—many skinks seem to hate having water drop onto their bodies) should be dechlorinated and have few minerals if you want to avoid white stains on the cage walls and fixtures.

**GUT-LOADING AND DUSTING**

Most keepers are in agreement that skinks, like other reptiles, need vitamin and calcium supplements if they are to remain healthy, grow well, and have a chance to reproduce. Traditionally a vitamin mixture produced specifically for reptiles has been added as either a liquid or a powder directly to the food, and calcium has been added in the form of special reptile calcium sources that have a proper balance of calcium and phosphorus. Bonemeal (without any additives) and ground oystershell or eggshell are natural calcium sources that have their followers, while many keepers prefer a more synthetic mix with calcium from several sources.

When feeding living insects, many keepers prefer to dust the insects with a fine vitamin and calcium mixture. This "shake and bake" method is quite simple. The insects, regardless of type, are very gently misted, just enough to moisten them, and placed in a plastic bag with a pinch of the

work well, are eaten greedily by the crickets, and are more convenient than mixing gut-loading supplements at home. When fed along with a bit of greens, they provide a balanced diet for crickets. Mealworms can be gut-loaded by adding supplements to their oatmeal or bran, but the technique does not work well with them.

## CRICKETS AND MEALWORMS

I won't go into much detail about culturing these insects, but

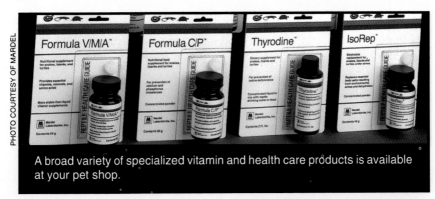

PHOTO COURTESY OF MARDEL

A broad variety of specialized vitamin and health care products is available at your pet shop.

vitamin-calcium mix. The bag is twisted shut, enclosing an air pocket, and then gently shaken until the insects become whitish with the powder. Feed at once.

Gut-loading works well with crickets. It consists of feeding the crickets food that contains a large amount of a vitamin and calcium mixture. Over the course of a day or two of feeding, the guts of the crickets accumulate high levels of the supplements, which are passed on to the lizards that feed on them. Commercial cricket foods are available in your pet shop that are designed especially for gut-loading crickets. They

you ought to know the basics. Live insects are not always available at your pet shop, especially during the winter, and it is always good to have a culture at home to fall back on if you can't get the insects at the shop. Additionally, culturing at home produces a variety of sizes of insects to accommodate different sizes and ages of skinks.

Mealworms can be cultured in a sweater box, large waxed ice cream carton, old leaky aquarium, or any other suitable container of a gallon (4 liters) or more in volume. The lid should be ventilated so the contents stay dry (fungus is always a problem in mealworm cultures). Fill the container about half full of oatmeal or bran and add a bit of bonemeal or chicken laying mash to increase the calcium content of the worms (actually larvae of a big black beetle, *Tenebrio molitor*). Some pieces of cardboard provide egg-laying spots for the adults. A few dozen mealworms are added to the mix, the container is covered, and the colony is left to itself for a month. By then the larvae will have matured into adults that are laying eggs and there should be at least some small larvae present. At room temperature it takes about six days for the eggs to hatch and about two months for the larvae to mature into pupae; the adults emerge from their pupal skins after another two to four weeks. Different strains of mealworms seem to have very different generation times from egg to adult, and the large species being sold as giant mealworms seem to be especially slow in maturing and hard to cultivate. Stick to ordinary small mealworms for your skinks. Very pale mealworms (almost white) have recently shed and are softer than more brownish specimens, thus better to feed to small skinks.

Never use mealworms as a main diet for your lizards. They are a good treat and a good food item for those periods when crickets are not available.

Crickets are available in all sizes from many pet shops. Adults will be taken by most skinks, while micros or pin-heads may be neces-sary for small species and the young of larger species. Shop-purchased pinheads often have very high mortality rates because they are very delicate animals. Crickets have to be kept at fairly high temperatures (best at 80°F, 27°C, and higher) to go through a generation in a reasonable time (12 to 15 weeks). If you just need adult crickets to feed to your skinks, you are better off pur-chasing them as needed; if you need small crickets, you are better off culturing them.

Put a group of adult crickets (males will sing and females can be recognized by their long saber-shaped ovipositor projecting from

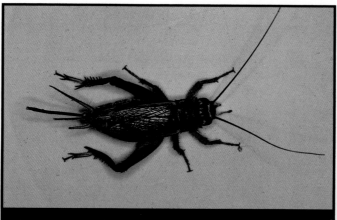

M. GILROY

Almost every pet shop carries crickets, which will be the staple food of your skinks. Even baby skinks will accept pinhead crickets.

M. ROBERTS

Mealworms are easy to culture in limited space. The common species does well at room temperature, but the giants need a higher temperature. Most pet shops carry mealworms.

the center of the tail) into a roomy (5 or 10 gallons, 20 to 40 liters) aquarium or plastic terrarium that can be securely covered with fine screen (to prevent escapes). The bottom of the tank should contain about 3 inches of fine, moist sand, and the sand must be kept moist (not wet) by daily misting. A shallow bowl should contain a sponge that is washed each day and kept wet—crickets need drinking water to survive but will drown in an open bowl. You can also make a drinking bottle for the crickets by filling a small bottle with water and then adding a wick of blotter paper or cotton that completely fills the neck of the bottle so crickets cannot enter. Provide dishes of cricket food from the pet shop and a few bits of lettuce and perhaps an apple core or two as food. Cover should be present; torn pieces of paper egg cartons, toilet paper

rolls, and coils of corrugated cardboard about 3 inches high work well.

Almost immediately the female crickets will begin to lay literally thousands of eggs in the sand, and they will continue to lay until they die in about three or four weeks. Of course, the adults can be gradually fed to your skinks after about the first week and you still will have thousands of tiny crickets hatching out in about three to four weeks at 80°F (27°C). By the time the crickets start hatching, all the adults must be gone from the tank. The tiny crickets should be given fresh food dishes, a shallow, safe water sponge, and bits of lettuce, as well as fresh hiding places. (All the old hiding places will be covered with cricket pellets that could pass on diseases.) The microcrickets grow slowly and have a tendency to eat each other, but you still should

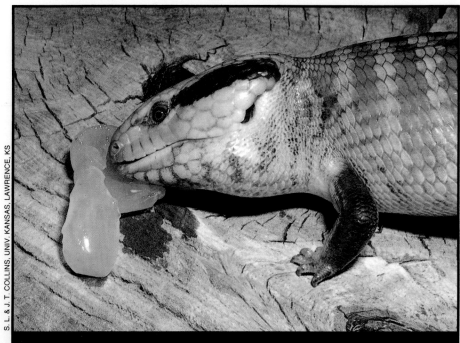

S. L. & J. T. COLLINS, UNIV. KANSAS, LAWRENCE, KS

Never pass up more unusual foods for your skinks. Australian blue-tongues (as *Tiliqua scincoides* above) often prefer fruits, such as grapes, while insect larvae of all types will be taken by most skinks (as *Egernia depressa* below).

J. MERLI

have a few thousand pieces of food for baby skinks. In some three to four months the crickets will be adults and can be used to start a new tank. Be sure to use all new materials in the new breeding tank, including fresh sand or at least sand that has been allowed to "weather" outdoors for a few weeks.

It never hurts to have a cricket colony as a back-up for problems at the local pet shop. Winter is especially hard on shipments of crickets, and so are the hot days of midsummer. I personally like the chirping of crickets, but many people go quietly insane listening to dozens of crickets singing away for hours at a time, day in and day out. The choice is yours.

Large skinks have heavy jaws and strong jaw muscles, and most will not hesitate to bite when annoyed. Most can produce only a painful pinch, but some, like this Shingleback, *Trachydosaurus rugosus*, could cause minor damage.

K. H. SWITAK

K. H. SWITAK

*Eumeces skiltonianus*, the Western Skink, often is locally common in the western United States and makes an excellent pet.

# NORTH AMERICAN SKINKS

Tropical America has relatively few skinks, mostly a few species of *Mabuya* and *Sphenomorphus* that extend north into southern Mexico. The North American skink fauna is comprised mostly of species of *Eumeces*, over a dozen species being found in the United States and several more restricted to mostly northern and central Mexico. Additionally, the small brown species of *Scincella* (formerly *Lygosoma*) range from the southern United States, where the species *S. laterale*, the Ground Skink, probably is the most abundant and widely distributed lizard, south into Mexico. Florida is home to an additional genus of skink, the small, worm-like *Neoseps reynoldsi*, a strange sand-swimmer with greatly reduced legs and a flattened snout. *Neoseps* was not described until 1910 and makes a poor pet, though it has been noted to feed on termites in captivity. *Scincella laterale* also is hard to keep because of its small size and requirement for moist or wet litter in which to burrow; it dries out easily and usually starves to death in a few days.

In North America your choice usually is a species of *Eumeces*, with the five-lined skinks (*E. laticeps*, the Broadhead Skink; *E. inexpectatus*, the Southeastern Five-lined Skink; and *E. fasciatus*, the true Five-lined Skink) being the most commonly collected for the pet market. In most parts of the United States (except the Northeast) it is easy to collect one

Though an adult in size (about 9 inches long), this Broadhead Skink, *Eumeces laticeps*, still retains the juvenile pattern, including a mostly blue tail. Probably the pattern will change by next spring.

or two specimens of the common local *Eumeces*, and they are all much alike in general keepability. The drier western states have some very attractive species that tend to be found in moist meadows at higher elevations, few skinks being common in the desert. The Coal Skink, *Eumeces anthracinus*, occasionally is sold but seems to be an exceptional species that requires cool surroundings and generally does poorly in captivity.

To identify North American skinks consult a good field guide. The typical skink is 6 to 10 inches long when adult and glossy brownish above, with a dark brown stripe along the side from the eye into the base of the tail. Usually a thin whitish stripe demarks the upper (and sometimes lower) edge of the brown stripe, and in the five-lined skinks the two white stripes on each side are joined by another (the fifth) stripe running from the head to the tail down the center of the back. Juveniles and females of the three species of five-lines are remarkably similar in all respects, differing in minor details of scale size under the tail (an enlarged central row in the Five-lined and Broadhead, no enlarged row in

Though the Ground Skink, *Scincella laterale*, is attractive and abundant, it makes a poor pet and is not suggested for the beginning keeper.

R. T. ZAPPALORTI

G. PISANI

The southwestern United States and adjacent Mexico have several interesting skinks that seldom are kept in the terrarium. This is *Eumeces callicephalus*, the Mountain Skink.

the Southeastern), head scales, and scales under the toes. Hatchlings of all three five-lines are very similar, being about 2.5 inches long and almost black, with five strongly contrasting bright white to yellow stripes over the body. The tail is brilliant iridescent blue.

As they grow, the young skinks gradually become dark brown, then glossy brown, the stripes fading to cream and the stripe on the center of the back often becoming indistinct (though usually visible at least behind the head). The tail fades from blue to bluish gray and may eventually become uniformly brown to grayish brown. Male five-lined skinks become almost uniformly glossy brown, but in the breeding season (about April to June) the sides of the head become bright red. Males are extremely aggressive at this time and should never be trusted with juveniles. Commonly five-lines live for six to eight years, with occasional specimens attaining ages over 12.

Keeping the five-lined skinks in captivity is simple, and they make excellent pets for beginners. Because the true Five-lined Skink (*E. fasciatus*) is rare in Florida, the common five-line on the market (at least those coming from Florida) is the Southeastern Five-line. This species usually is 7 to 8 inches long when adult, the males somewhat longer than the females. Southeastern Five-lines tolerate quite dry situations and like it warm, but they do well in

R. D. BARTLETT

An adult Broadhead Skink, *Eumeces laticeps*, displaying colors typical of a gravid female. Notice that the lips are pale yellowish cream with no traces of the red coloration typical of adult males. Broadheads often bask and climb well, features unusual in the five-lined skinks. This species makes an inexpensive, excellent pet.

the temperate litter terrarium described earlier. Though they can climb, they seldom venture far from the ground when in captivity. Crickets and other insects form the major food in the terrarium, with some individuals displaying a taste for fruit and babyfood. For all practical purposes *E. fasciatus* is identical in keepability to the Southeastern Five-line.

Somewhat different is the Broadhead Skink, *E. laticeps*, the giant of the group. Females are like the Southeastern Five-line, but males are much larger than male Southeastern Five-lines (to a full foot in length), with exceptionally heavy jowls. They are glossy brown with a bright red head during the mating season (only tinged with red after early summer). Unlike the other five-lines, Broadheads like to climb and often are found basking in full sun on stumps and fence posts, and they like large, sturdy climbing branches in the terrarium. Big males can be hard biters (personal experience) and unbelievably aggressive. Even in nature they sometimes are found eating overripe fruit, and in the terrarium they will take almost anything. Never cage small Broadheads with adult males— these skinks will regenerate lost tails, but they do not regenerate lost feet and legs, not to mention heads. Big males perhaps are best given their own terraria except during the breeding season.

*Eumeces* species seem to breed in much the same fashion wherever they are found in the temperate forests of the Northern Hemisphere, whether in the Carolinas or Japan. The species hibernate from about October or November through most of March, emerging with the spring thaw. Adults bask a great deal and feed heavily for about a month, when mating occurs. Males actively chase females and wrestle them into position, using the heavy jaws to bite the neck and shoulders of the female. (Mature females of many skinks sometimes can be recognized by scars on the neck from previous matings.) The male inserts one hemipenis into the female's cloaca. A female may mate with several males over a few weeks in May and early June, but after she is satisfactorily mated she no longer pays attention to males and may actively attack them.

Three or four weeks after mating, the female scoops out a shallow depression under a rock or log and lays about 6 to 15 oval

Mole Skinks, *Eumeces egregius*, of the southeastern United States are elongated burrowers with bright red or blue tails. They can be very difficult to maintain.

R. S. SIMMONS

white eggs with somewhat elastic shells. *E. fasciatus* and *E. inexpectatus* typically have clutches of six to nine eggs, while *E. laticeps* lays a dozen or so. The female coils around her eggs under the log or rock and guards them, even staying in place if the log is overturned by a collector. She will eat small insects, snails, and other prey that passes by but does little or no active hunting for the 30 to 60 days required for the eggs to hatch. When the young emerge they quickly scatter into the litter and the mother goes about her business. Occasionally five-lined skinks mate a second time and lay a second batch of eggs, but only if the temperature and humidity allowed the first batch to develop rapidly.

The brilliant blue tail of the young lasts for over a year,

*Eumeces fasciatus* is THE five-lined skink over much of the eastern United States. This young specimen still shows the very dark, almost black, body color typical of the first year of life.

R. D. BARTLETT

An adult male Broadhead Skink, *Eumeces laticeps*, is quite different from young and females. He lacks all traces of striping on the body and for at least a couple of months each year has a bright red head, including the lips.

beginning to brown-up by the lizard's second year of life. Research has shown that the blue tail of the young serves as a behavioral modifier of adult male behavior. Although the males will snap at any other small lizard, especially when they are in the mating mood and show reddish heads, they will not snap at lizards displaying bright blue tails. This reduces juvenile mortality while allowing adults and young to forage in the same areas, taking different sizes of prey.

Like almost all other skinks, the tails of *Eumeces* break off when the lizard is disturbed or grabbed. Tail loss is under somewhat voluntary control and always takes place at the same position, through one of the vertebrae where there is a special constriction to allow easy breaking. The muscles and blood vessels at this plane of autotomy (the technical name for loss of the tail) constrict to prevent blood loss. Because the tail continues to wriggle after it is loss, it helps divert the attention of predators for a few seconds so the skink can

R. D. BARTLETT

A variety of North American skinks. **Top:** A baby Great Plains Skink, *Eumeces obsoletus*. **Center:** An adult male Southeastern Five-lined Skink, *E. inexpectatus*. **Bottom:** A Four-lined Skink, *E. tetragrammus*.

R. D. BARTLETT

P. FREED

escape into the litter. The tail that regenerates is shorter, dull in color, and less flexible than the original because it is a mostly cartilaginous rod lacking true vertebrae. In populations where predation from skunks and other animals is high, it may be almost impossible to find adults with collection, a large (over a foot in big males) species that likes it a bit drier and rockier than the five-lines. Its young are black with white spots on the lips and a bluish tail, while the heavy-set adults are dark and bronzy brown with yellowish side and belly, in some ways reminiscent of a

R. D. BARTLETT

An adult Great Plains Skink, *Eumeces obsoletus*, is an impressive animal. The oblique rows of spots on the sides are distinctive among North American skinks.

complete original tails.

If you attempt to collect your own skinks as pets, first be sure that it is legal in your area. Though five-lines and related species may be abundant in many areas, they may still be legally protected and you may need a license or permit to collect and keep them. Always know your local laws before you touch anything. If you live in the central western United States you might be able to add a Great Plains Skink, *Eumeces obsoletus*, to your collection, a large (over a foot in Berber Skink from northern Africa. Gilbert's Skinks (*E. gilberti*) and Western Skinks (*E. skiltonianus*) are the typical smaller skinks of the western United States and look much like five-lines that lack the central line down the back and are a bit more elongated. In some forms of Gilbert's Skink the tail of the young is bright red, while some forms of the Western Skink retain the bright blue tail into the adult. Both make decent pets though secretive.

R. D. BARTLETT.

An adult male *Eumeces schneideri schneideri* is a gorgeous animal with a pleasing combination of orange and blue-gray colors. Notice the continuous orange stripe low on the body.

# AFRICAN SKINKS

The most commonly imported skinks for the terrarium hobby probably are those of Africa. This continent contains a vast array of habitats, from the driest deserts to the North through rainforests and swamps in the center, with cool plateaus and rocky savannahs to the South. At least five genera from these habitats find their way into the terrarium, several at very low prices for wild-caught adult specimens. One species is a mainstay of the skink trade, while the others are available seasonally or sporadically. We'll start with the Berber Skink, an old mainstay of the hobby.

## BERBER SKINKS, *EUMECES SCHNEIDERI*

These commonly imported skinks are the hulking giants of the inexpensive skinks. Though they are not as large or heavily built as the Australian blue-tongues, they are bigger (often 12 to 16 inches long) and bulkier than any other familiar skinks. Dwellers in the drier savannahs and deserts from northern Africa east to Pakistan, they are easily recognized by the combination of large size, a bright orange stripe along the upper lip and usually the lower side (especially obvious in  males), and three large comb-scales at the front of the ear

There is some controversy as to the temperament of *E. s. schneideri*. Some keepers say it is relatively gentle, others that it is a true beast.

R. D. BARTLETT.

opening that prevent sand from entering the ear during burrowing. Accomplished burrowers, they often are found under rock piles and in other animal burrows. Much of their day is spent basking at very high temperatures, building up the energy to chase down insects, and a balanced calcium supplement so there are no problems with vitamin D3 conversion. Be sure that a warm basking rock is available in one corner of the terrarium (use a dry desert setup, of course), where basking temperatures over 100°F (38°C) are fine. The other end of

The northwestern African subspecies or full species of Berber Skink, *Eumeces schneideri algeriensis*, has a distinctive pattern of white spots on the back and an indistinct orange stripe on the lower sides.

snails, small lizards, and even the occasional small mouse.

In captivity Berber Skinks feed on a variety of foods, from the usual crickets and mealworms through finely minced pieces of fruit and even a pinkie mouse on occasion. Many keepers have good luck with a diet containing all these ingredients plus a low-protein dog food. Liberal additions of powdered vitamins are essential. Be sure to provide the correct combination of UV lighting

the terrarium, preferably where most of the hideboxes and burrowing spots are located, should be allowed to stay cool, perhaps 75°F (24°C) during the day. This skink needs a strong temperature drop during the night, like it would have at home in the desert, so let the cool end of the terrarium drop to about 65°F (18°C) at night.

*Eumeces schneideri* is a variable lizard with a wide range, and it has been divided into several subspecies that differ in details of scalation and color pattern, as well as size. Recently these subspecies have in some cases been elevated to species rank, but only two are presently of interest to hobbyists. In the typical *E.*

*Eumeces* nastiness when more than one male is confined in the terrarium. From northwestern Africa comes *E. s. algeriensis*, which tends to lack the orange stripe along the side and has the orange spots of the back clustered

Female Berber Skinks (foreground) have relatively duller colors than males and are smaller. This is a pair of Algerian Berbers.

R. D. BARTLETT.

*schneideri schneideri* imported from northeastern Africa (especially Egypt), the orange stripe on the upper lip runs almost continuously along the side to the hind legs and the back is grayish with scattered orange spots. This subspecies is often seen in the hobby and is the form that has been most often kept in Europe. Though some hobbyists report that males of this form are exceptionally aggressive at all times, others note only the typical

into many narrow orange stripes on a brownish background. Females of both forms are duller than males and often lack orange entirely. *E. s. algeriensis* is supposed to have a much better temperament than the typical *schneideri*, but probably this is individually variable.

There is no doubt that the Berber Skink is a rough skink when mating. The large males may fight until one loses a leg or the tail, and even females may be bitten until they bleed. For this reason it is best to keep only a pair (distinguished by color intensity) in a large terrarium. Provide many hiding places and the usual water bowl. It might help to give each skink its own food bowl as well. Even young specimens should be watched carefully for signs of excessive aggression.

Breeding this skink in captivity is uncommon, actually almost unheard of. Most specimens seen in the hobby are males, which seem to be selectively collected (perhaps because they are more easily found). The skinks have to be exposed to shortened days and cooler nights for at least two months during the winter if you wish to have any chance at breeding success. Gradually drop the day length from 12 to 14 hours to six or so over a period of about eight weeks, from October through November. At the same time reduce the general terrarium temperature from about 85°F (30°C) to 65°F (18°C) during the day, letting it drop as low as 50°F (10°C) at night in the lizards's favorite burrowing spots. Hold the terrarium at these temperatures until late February, when you can gradually return to normal higher temperatures and longer day lengths. Clutches reported in

The flattened snout of the Sandfish, *Scincus scincus*, may be its most obvious feature, but the glossy tan and dark brown body pattern is very attractive. Like many desert skinks, the Sandfish is a "sand swimmer" that moves easily through loose sand.

W. P. MARA

*Chalcides ocellatus* is one of the more common African barrel skinks and has one of the most attractive patterns of the group. These are among the many skinks that give birth to living young.

captivity have been small, often only one to three eggs, but over a dozen are laid in nature. This skink is definitely worth breeding because it is long-lived (at least 20 years) and adaptable, and it is likely that various political, economic, and environmental problems in northern Africa eventually will reduce its availability to the hobby.

### SAND SKINKS

The deserts of Africa and the Middle East are difficult environments, but they are far from sterile. Among other things, they are home to many species of the long-bodied, small-legged barrel skinks, *Chalcides*, as well as a complex variety of sandfish species, *Scincus*, with flattened snouts. Various species of these genera are imported seasonally and can be kept much like Berber Skinks, but on a smaller scale. They feed well on crickets (gut-loaded or powdered with vitamins) and will take waxworms and mealworms as well as sometimes a bit of fruit. Sandfish, a recent pet "sensation," may stay buried in the dry part of the terrarium for days at a time, emerging only at night to feed. However, this is mostly because they are shy of human movement (transferred as vibrations through the sand). They still need to bask daily, so just leave them alone until they adjust to normal movements about the cage and be sure they always have access to warm basking spots.

The barrel skinks, unlike Berber Skinks, are mostly (perhaps all) livebearers, giving birth to young that look much like the adults. Because the adult size of species in this genus varies so greatly (from 6 to 20 inches), litter size varies as well, from two or three young to almost two dozen. Again unlike Berber Skinks, barrel skinks are not dependent on a seasonal cooling to reproduce successfully, mating occurring at almost any time of the year. Females usually carry their young for about three months before giving birth. Males are not especially aggressive, so small colonies can be kept in a terrarium of suitable size.

Sandfish are very stout-bodied skinks with short tails. At about 8 inches in length, they are large enough to take adult crickets and similar fare. One reference suggest that they not be given water bowls because of the possibility of drowning; I honestly don't know if this is necessary (I've seen them kept with water bowls), but it might be a wise precaution and they shouldn't really need much water. The front of the head is depressed and sometimes even spade-shaped, with the lower jaw countersunken and the ear opening almost closed by scales. These all are adaptations for burrowing in loose sand, a skill at which sandfish excel. They need the usual hot basking spots (100°F, 38°C) and cool corners of

R. D. BARTLETT

The true Fire Skink, *Lygosoma (Riopa) fernandi*, is certainly one of the most colorful of the skinks and can hold its own against most other lizards as well. The contrasting red sides and the black blotch over and before the front leg are good marks of the species, which often is confused with *Mabuya perroteti* and other skinks with somewhat reddish sides. This is a long-bodied burrower that can be kept much like North American *Eumeces*, though it seldom does well in captivity, perhaps because of stress during shipping.

other desert skinks. Like the barrel skinks, they give live birth, but so far they have rarely been bred in captivity.

At the moment it would seem that most or all sand skinks on the market are wild-caught, but at least the barrel skinks have some potential for forming captive-bred stocks. Species identification is difficult in both *Chalcides* and *Scincus*, so the help of experts may be necessary in identifying the species present in your terrarium.

## RIOPAS

After several years of near absence from the terrarium hobby, Fire Skinks, *Lygosoma (Riopa) fernandi*, seem to have made a return. These beautiful foot-long skinks from central Africa are glossy brown on the back and bright red on the sides, with narrow white vertical bars and broken black bars showing through the red. Long-bodied and short-legged, they are burrowers that can be kept in simple litter

R. D. BARTLETT

For many years Fire Skinks, *Lygosoma (Riopa) fernandi*, were hard to obtain, but recently they have become common, though only as wild-caught specimens at fairly high prices. *Riopa* often is used as a full genus, a matter of considerable debate among specialists.

terrarium setups like those used for five-lined skinks. They love to bask and will accept the usual array of insects and fruit-based foods. Even small specimens (the colors intensify with age and size) can be very expensive to purchase, and they seldom are bred in the terrarium.

The correct taxonomic name of these skinks is still uncertain, as it and its relatives have been switched back and forth from genus to genus for years. *Riopa* species have long, cylindrical bodies, short legs (often almost absent), and long tails. Some species have spectacular patterns, but most are rare and poorly known burrowers found from Africa through much of tropical Asia. *Lygosoma* is a massive genus containing a variety of sizes and types of skinks, though most are slender-bodied and have reduced legs. This type of skink is nearly worldwide in distribution (the Ground Skink of the southern U.S. once was placed in *Lygosoma*, for instance) and has confused taxonomists for decades. Currently *Riopa* is considered to be a synonym or subgenus of *Lygosoma*, but don't be surprised if it is returned to full generic rank in the near future. Nothing ever stays the same in taxonomy.

## MABUYAS

African five-lined skinks and rainbow skinks can be any of two dozen or more species of *Mabuya* imported sporadically for the terrarium trade. The species in your dealer's cages may vary from month to month depending on who is shipping, so mabuyas are a great buy for the keeper with a flare to the unknown. As a general rule, mabuyas are kept much like five-lined skinks, though most prefer it a bit drier and warmer. They love to bask on mounds of rock. Most species are similar to *Eumeces* in general size (6 to 12 inches) and shape and have patterns including pale and dark stripes, often with tiny white or greenish spots, and sometimes with blue tails even in the adults. Males commonly have reddish heads and a red tinge on the lower sides. Mabuyas have ridged scales, while ridges are absent or nearly so in *Eumeces* species. They'll eat almost anything you would feed to a five-lined.

Mabuyas can be egg-layers or livebearers. It seems that this varies not only from species to species, but may also differ among populations of a single species. Males may aggressively court females much like the five-lines. Since there is almost no way to identify mabuyas, provide a nesting site under a log or flat rock if you see mating behavior. If

P. FREED

The Kalahari Tree Skink, *Mabuya spilogaster*, of the Namib Desert is one of literally dozens of mabuyas that could appear in the pet shop on occasion.

the female disappears a few weeks after mating, she probably is guarding a nest of whitish eggs. The young usually have bright blue tails and are darker than adults, again as in the five-lines.

Other African skinks are imported on occasion, but they can be kept either like five-lines or like Berber Skinks, depending on their natural habitat. Identification can be difficult or almost impossible even with the use of modern field guides. African skinks have much potential in the hobby if various political and economic problems do not interfere.

R. D. BARTLETT

Notice the fringe of scales in front of the ear opening in both the *Eumeces schneideri algeriensis* above and the *Mabuya perroteti* below. Such scales help prevent the entry of sand into the ear in burrowing animals. Photo above: M. Gilroy.

# ASIAN SKINKS

Though Asia has hundreds of species of skinks, few are found with any regularity in the terrarium hobby. This is due in part to the dull nature of most Asian skinks. The average Asian skink is a small *Sphenomorphus*, *Lygosoma*, or *Emoia* species, under 6 inches long, with short legs, a dark stripe on each side, and usually dark spots on the back. This general pattern covers dozens of species that are litter-dwellers feeding on small insects. They are seldom imported and usually are too fragile to do well in the terrarium. Several riopas are described from the continent, some with very interesting and distinctive patterns, but they appear to be rare and virtually never collected. Only three genera of small Asian skinks appear regularly in the hobby, but they are overshadowed by the giant Monkey Skink of the Solomons, which we'll treat as Asian to make this chapter of decent size.

## RAINBOW SKINKS

The genus *Mabuya* occurs in Asia as well as Africa, and several species are exported from Indonesia and perhaps Thailand. The most commonly seen species (I've no idea what name to give it) is glossy iridescent brown, sometimes with hints of blue on the tail and bright multicolor shimmers over the body in the right light. Some species have traces of pale stripes on the body and some have small white spots. One species has a distinct greenish tinge. Keep these common and inexpensive skinks like five-lines in a litter terrarium and they should do well. At least one Asian rainbow skink is a livebearer, but there is no guarantee that the species you breed will not be an egg-layer. These are gorgeous first skinks for a beginner if you are careful to get a specimen that is not stressed from poor shipping conditions. Check for loose skin around the pelvis and hind legs, a sign of a skink on the way out. Like other imported lizards, rainbow skinks may have heavy intestinal worm loads, but unfortunately their low cost makes veterinary attention prohibitive for most keepers. Your pet shop should be able to recommend an appropriate dose of Flagyl or some other general-purpose reptile wormer that can be used with caution.

## GREEN TREE SKINKS

This stunning medium-sized (about 9 to 11 inches long) skink is readily recognized by its bright green head and anterior body. The legs are long and strong, the tail is longer than the head and body length, and the snout is tapered to a rather narrow blunt point fitted for poking into cracks and crevices in branches and logs. Now known as *Lamprolepis smaragdina*, the Green Tree Skink has smooth, glossy scales that help distinguish it from the coarser, rough-scaled tree skinks of the closely related genus *Dasia*. The species ranges widely over tropical Asia (including New Guinea and the Solomons) and differs quite a bit in details of

K. H. SWITAK

Green Tree Skinks, *Lamprolepis smaragdina*, are among the most uniquely colored of all skinks and are fairly common in the pet trade. The narrow snout helps this arboreal skink seek out insects from cracks under bark.

R. D. BARTLETT

color pattern from population to population. Some have only the head bright green, the rest of the body being brown with rows of squarish blackish spots along the upper sides, while others have almost the entire body bright green, the color even extending onto the tail.

In the terrarium this is an

will feed on a variety of insects, especially crickets and mealworms, and also takes flies on a regular basis. It lays eggs that it places in decaying vegetation on the ground or in a hole in a rotting branch.

The Green Tree Skink is an interesting pet lizard that certainly is different in both color

W. WUSTER

*Mabuya multifasciata* is one of the several widely distributed Asian species of the genus that are imported on a sporadic basis. Males sometimes have reddish sides.

active species that likes to climb and constantly is investigating each little crack or niche for insects. It likes to bask early in the day and likes a relatively high humidity. Provide a tall terrarium with firmly anchored climbing branches and perhaps a few bromeliads or other epiphytic plants to appease its curiosity. It

and behavior from the run of the mill species. Though hardy, it rarely breeds in the terrarium and captive-bred stock is presently unavailable. However, its size and broad range indicate that it should be possible to adapt it to the terrarium sufficiently to establish captive-bred stocks if the hobbyist is willing to spend the time on the species and give it a large terrarium. Sexes should be distinguishable by behavior (color has nothing to do with sex, by the way, in this species).

## WATERSIDE SKINKS

The first time you see a waterside skink, *Tropidophorus*, in the pet shop, you'll have to stare at it a bit to make sure it really is a skink. They are fairly large animals, some 8 to 12 inches long when adult (most in the shops seem to be immatures), with the scales of the neck, back, and tail variously keeled. In the most commonly seen types the keels are high and bluntly pointed, giving the lizard a very "primitive" appearance. The head scales may or may not be keeled. Often the tip of the tail is missing or regenerated. Color patterns vary quite a bit, but usually it is brownish with darker brown crossbars and spots; there may be a dark spot over the base of the front leg.

Waterside skinks are ground-dwellers that like streambeds and other humid areas in rainforests. They swim well and will take to the water when threatened. They spend much of the day hiding under rocks and logs and are not great baskers, though they should always have a basking rock available. Keep the terrarium humid and warm and provide a

An especially rugged species of waterside skink, *Tropidophorus* sp., supposedly from the Philippines. These unusual skinks have only recently been seen on a regular basis in the pet shops.

R. D. BARTLETT

W.P. MARA

Waterside skink. Ventral view of an unidentified species possibly from Thailand.

water bowl that might be used for more than just drinking.

Waterside skinks have a spotty history in the terrarium hobby and have never been common, though not especially expensive. They may prove to be more delicate than most hobbyists can handle, because they certainly are specialized. Waterside skinks give livebirth to about 6 to 12 young that resemble their parents, but almost nothing seems to be recorded about their mating habits. The species occur south to Australia but even there are not well-known. If you need a good challenge in a skink, a waterside may be just up your alley.

Waterside skink, *Tropidophorus thai*, a species that at least in the juvenile has an interesting color scheme.

W. WUSTER

W. P. MARA

Close-up of the head of *Tropidophorus* showing the strongly keeled scales at the back of the head.

## MONKEY SKINKS

Ten years ago *Corucia zebrata* was just a name for a virtually unknown skink as far as even the most advanced hobbyist was concerned. Today you can special-order one from almost any specialty pet shop, and some shops even stock them on occasion. In fact, this is one of the most commonly photographed skinks today, and it is possible to find more literature on it than on any other single species of hobby skink. Yet for some reason it does not yet have a uniform common name. It has been called Solomons Islands Giant Skin, Monkey-tailed Skink, Prehensile-

The unique Monkey Skink, *Corucia zebrata*, still is a problematic species for most keepers.

R. G. SPRACKLAND

This attractive greenish patterned Monkey Skink is just one of five or six major color patterns in the species, some of which may be restricted to specific areas of the Solomons.

R. D. BARTLETT

tailed Skink, and varying combinations of these names. For convenience I'll just call it the Monkey Skink—at least it's a short name.

This is the largest known species of skink, with a maximum total length of about 32 inches, about two-thirds of this a relatively slender but very strong and muscular tail. The tail is prehensile, able to firmly wrap around branches and act as a fifth legs (as in many South American monkeys, thus the common name). The deep head features a large scale over the snout and very large nostrils. The eyes often are bright orange. The legs are long and very strong, as

you might expect of a species that spends most of its life in the trees.

Found through much of the Solomon Islands, *Corucia zebrata* is a variable lizard. Generally adults are some shade of olive tan to bright green, with black or dark brown speckling over the back and sometimes broad oblique dark brown bars. Some specimens have bright yellow heads as adults, while newborns often have overall yellow or even orange tinges. It has been suggested that some color patterns are typical of certain islands in the Solomons chain, but so far there has been little published to back this up. Typical adults are over 24 inches in length. As might be expected of

P. FREED

A mother Monkey Skink, *Corucia zebrata*, and her recently born young. There are many observations indicating that mothers may care for their young for months or perhaps even years after their birth. Twins are fairly common in this species.

a lizard this size, they can pack a mean bite and can scratch as well, though usually they are very calm, even gentle, lizards that do not object to handling.

Monkey Skinks are unusual not only in appearance but in behavior. First, they are largely nocturnal, active from sunset to sunrise, though they may sleep in plain sight during the day. This means that they do not necessarily need a broad-spectrum light or a basking light in their cage, though most keepers feel that providing a broad-spectrum lamp for at least eight hours a day is certainly not harmful and may help keep the animals healthy. Since they should be kept in a heavily planted terrarium, lighting is essential for the health of the plants anyway. It also means that their food should be presented at dusk.

Second, they are almost strictly arboreal, spending all their time in the branches. Though they can move around on the ground, they prefer the branches. This means they need a tall terrarium with lots of branches and preferably living plants. It is not unusual to see a Monkey Skink hanging by its tail and one leg while calmly reaching for another branch. They need lots of hiding places both in the branches and on the ground to feel secure.

Third, Monkey Skinks are vegetarians. As far as known, they do not need any animal protein in their diet, feeding on a variety of fruits, vegetables, and greens in captivity. In nature they seem to feed mostly on the young shoots of a specific vine, and in the terrarium they enjoy the shoots of pothos and similar plants. Feed every second day on a good salad of bananas, kiwi, green peas, diced melon, stringbeans, diced pears, fresh spinach, and similar items. Some keepers have had good luck with an artificial diet of fruit babyfoods (sweet potato has been strongly recommended), canned yams, and high-quality monkey biscuits. Some specimens, especially wild-caught (yes, most specimens in the shops still are wild-caught), never feed sufficiently in captivity. These skinks exhibit coprophagy, the eating of their own feces, an act that may be vital in producing the proper gut flora and fauna in young skinks and may have something to do with maintenance of the correct vitamin levels in the body. Just ignore the practice—it's natural and harmless and helps keep the cage clean.

To keep Monkey Skinks you need a very large terrarium (at least 3 to 5 feet on a side) that is high enough to allow for plenty of climbing. Two males in a terrarium can fight to the death, so keep just a single skink in an enclosure unless you are trying to breed them. Sexes are almost impossible to distinguish, though males have heavier jowls than females and usually have a bulge at the base of the tail caused by the hemipenes. The temperature should not exceed 85°F (30°C), and preferably should be about 75°F (24°C), dropping about 10 degrees at night. Maintain a humidity of at least 70%. Commonly the bottom of the terrarium is covered with a deep layer of moss to help maintain the humidity and the terrarium is misted heavily every two or three days. The skinks drink from water dripping from leaves and do not like to be actually wet down with the spray. A water bowl will not be used for drinking. Again, provide many hiding places all over the terrarium.

Mating is rare in the terrarium, though births from gravid imported females are not uncommon. It seems that a cycle of two or three months in a relatively dry terrarium (especially during the late winter) followed by a drenching "rain" may initiate mating behavior. Mating itself seems to take place right at sunset. The exact gestation period still is unknown but seems to be about six or seven months. A female usually gives birth to one or two young about 10 to 12 inches in total length, but up to four young are recorded. It seems that in nature (and sometimes in the terrarium) a female and her young stay together for a long period and they may protect a territory and each other. Males definitely are known to be territorial in nature, defending a spot high in a tree against all intruders. I've seen no information on how long it takes a Monkey Skink to reach maturity, but it can be assumed to be over a year. These skinks live at least ten years in captivity and may be much longer-lived under the proper circumstances.

Animals this large and expensive deserve considerable forethought before purchase, including finding a veterinarian who is able to work on the various infections and wounds that these skinks tend to accumulate. A broad variety of diseases, infections, uterine problems, and even mouthrot have been described for Monkey Skinks, all of which need veterinary attention or could lead to death.

Though fascinating and easily available if you have the money, Monkey Skinks are not for the beginning hobbyist. They are fun to look at in the pet shop or in someone else's collection, but their care is so specialized that you need considerable experience and luck to keep them successfully.

Pink-tongued Skinks, *Tiliqua gerrardi*, are among the most interesting Australian skinks. They are more elongated and longer-tailed than most of the common blue-tongues of the same genus and do quite well in the terrarium.

W. P. MARA

# AUSTRALIAN SKINKS

Australia is a paradise for skink-lovers. It has a tremendous and diverse fauna that includes very large species *(Tiliqua* and *Egernia)* as well as many small species and species with reduced legs. Recently the Australian skinks have been revised repeatedly by several workers and many new species have been described as well as much learned about the ecology of many species. To hobbyists, however, Australian skinks mean the spiny-tailed skinks of the genus *Egernia* and the blue-tongues (and occasional pink-tongues) of the genus *Tiliqua*. Both these genera are comprised of species found in dry, almost desert-like environments as well as some found in the rainforests of the eastern coast. *Egernia* sometimes are very normal-looking lizards with just weak keels on the scales of the tail; the fourth toe is much longer than the third, as in most lizards. *Tiliqua* often have short tails (not true for the Pink-tongued Skink and its relatives) and always have heavy heads; the genus has the fourth toe about the same length as the third, never distinctly longer. In some *Tiliqua* the legs are small relative to the sausage-like body, and the lizard moves with a snake-like wriggle.

One species of each genus occurs in New Guinea and adjacent Indonesian territory, which may prove lucky for hobbyists. Currently Australia (and Papua New Guinea, for that matter) have strict laws prohibiting or at least tremendously restricting trade in these skinks. These laws do not apply to Indonesia, which is busily cutting down its forests and selling off any animals that survive long enough to enter the pet trade. Thus *Egernia frerei* and *Tiliqua gigas* have entered the commercial terrarium trade recently. Unfortunately, some exporters seem to be using these names to ship illegally collected Australian skinks under false papers, or at least this seems to be the explanation for the sudden discovery of several Australian endemics in Indonesian territory where they never were known before and are unlikely to exist in nature. Caution is advised whenever considering purchasing any of these lizards. Make sure the dealer has all the correct permits and they make sense. If you buy an illegal blue-tongue, the law may consider you to be just as guilty as the exporter and importer.

## SPINY-TAILED SKINKS

The 25 or more species of *Egernia* vary tremendously in appearance, but hobbyists are interested mostly in two or three extremely spiny species and a couple that are almost smooth. The smoothest species usually available is White's Skink, *E. whiti,* a 14-inch glossy brown lizard marked with dark-edged white spots. It is from dry forests and savannahs of southeastern Australia. About the same size is Cunningham's Skink, *E.*

R. D. BARTLETT

The Pygmy Spiny Skink, *Egernia depressa*, is a true gem of a spiny skink. One of the most desirable of the Australian species, it does well in the terrarium and often is bred, but it is quite expensive and probably beyond the budget of the beginner, as are most Australian skinks.

*cunninghami,* also of southeastern Australia but more typical of rocky terrain. Cunningham's Skink has most of the scales with low but obvious keels that project as low spines on the tail. Young specimens are covered with fine white spots that often become less distinct in adults.

Two extremely spiny *Egernias* are in the hobby and are among the most sough-after skinks. Both are rather flattened in shape and have short, broad tails only about a third of the body length and edged with large spines. The Gidgee Skink, *E. stokesi*, is fairly large, often reaching 9 or 10 inches in length, and tends to be dark dirty brown or grayish brown in color; the scales on top of the head are regular, not broken into small fragments, and there is only a single large spine (and sometimes a small second one) on each scale on the top of the tail. The Pygmy Spiny Skink, *E. depressa*, is similar at first glance but seldom exceeds 6 inches in total length and often is quite bright in color; the scales on top of the head are broken into irregular fragments, and there are three distinct spines on each tail scale.

The spiny-tailed skinks generally are kept in small colonies in roomy, dry terraria with lots of basking rocks and hiding places. Males often are extremely quarrelsome—downright mean, actually—and must be watched carefully to prevent serious accidents. They feed on the usual assortment of insects (occasionally with a pinkie mouse for variety in the larger species) and also nibble on fruit; some will take babyfood and dog food. Be sure to provide the usual vitamin and calcium supplements as well as both broad-spectrum fluorescents and basking lights. Females give live birth to usually one to three young about a third the length of the parent after a gestation period of about three to four months. These are slow-growing skinks that take at least three years to become sexually mature and might live 15 or more years in captivity.

### PINK-TONGUED SKINKS

*Tiliqua gerrardi* is the only commonly-seen species of the long-tailed *Tiliqua*s, forms in which the tail is at least as long as the head plus body length. The body is elongated and rather slender, and there often appears to be a distinct neck behind the squarish head. The coloration is simple, brown with darker oblique bars, and there usually are two dark brown bars below the eye. Unlike the more typical members of the genus, the tongue is bright pink. Adults commonly are 15 to 18 inches long.

Pink-tongues are rainforest lizards of southeastern Australia, living both on the ground and climbing on low branches; the

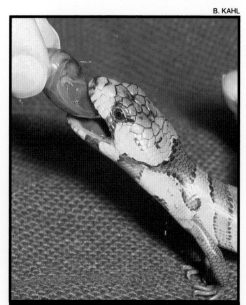

B. KAHL

The species of *Tiliqua* tend to be omnivorous in their diet, eating mostly insects but also enjoying fruits, veggies, and greens. Pink-tongues, *T. gerrardi*, are noted for their fondness for living snails.

long tail is prehensile, by the way. It feeds on a variety of insects and on snails during its nightly rambles—unlike most *Tiliqua*, the Pink-tongue is nocturnal or at least crepuscular (active at dawn and dusk). Be sure the terrarium is large enough that the lizards in it don't have to come into contact with each other, as this can be a mean species. Keep the terrarium moist by providing moss pads on the bottom, and make sure there are plenty of hiding places.

Captive-breeding of the Pink-tongue can be very productive and is not uncommon. In fact, most specimens are from several generations of captive-bred stock. A female gives birth to about 20 to 25 4-inch young after a gestation period of as much as

150 days. Unfortunately, the skinks may not breed each year and they take almost three years to become sexually mature. This currently is the most affordable *Tiliqua* on the market; in my opinion it also is the most attractive. Remember that it can be very quarrelsome, like the species of *Tiliqua* the tongue is large, very flexible, and bright blue against a pinkish or bright red mouth lining. Though these lizards are captive-bred today and easily available, they are too expensive for the average beginner to even consider, although wild-caught imports of the Indonesian

K. H. SWITAK

One of the more uncommon blue-tongues is *Tiliqua multifasciata*, the Centralian Blue-tongue. This female looks like she will give birth any day now. Note the many brown bands on the body and the dark band back from the eye.

other species of its genus, and it should not be hard to keep.

## BLUE-TONGUED SKINKS

When the average hobbyist thinks of a blue-tongued skink, the immediate impression is of a gigantic (often 24 inches long), very heavily built (a sausage on short legs) brown skink with a very short, smooth tail. In these

*T. gigas* sometimes are reasonably priced. If you purchase a blue-tongue, be sure that you arrange for veterinary supervision first because blue-tongues are investments as well as pets.

The most common Australian species, *T. scincoides*, the Eastern Blue-tongue, has very specific basking requirements, because it needs to function at an internal body temperature of over 80°F (27°C), so it must have both a basking rock at a temperature of about 100°F (38°C) and a cool corner of about 75°F (24°C) into which to retreat when the temperature becomes too high. Similar requirements are needed for most other large blue-tongues. Usually these species are maintained in large enclosures

for at least 8 to 12 hours per day. They will feed on a wide variety of insects and fruit, many specimens actually preferring fruit and vegetable salad to crickets. Give the widest variety of food possible and be sure to provide supplements regularly.

Like the other large skinks, these are quarrelsome animals and it may not be safe to include

K. H. SWITAK

*Tiliqua branchialis* of western Australia is one of the more poorly known species of the genus, but it does occasionally appear in the hobby.

that are kept dry (sometimes with a moist section included just for safety) except for water bowls. There must be many hiding places and of course basking spots. These are day-active (diurnal) skinks, though they often are active well into the evening, so provide broad-spectrum lighting

two males in even the largest enclosures. Keep a careful eye on the skinks and separate the animals if fights are noticed. Young skinks are especially at risk and may be injured by adults of both sexes. Males chase the females before mating. As expected, the blue-tongues give livebirth, with typical litters of one to perhaps a dozen common, depending on species, conditions, and individual variation. Gestation may take as little as three months or as much as six. The young grow fairly fast and are

## SHINGLEBACK SKINKS

Although it is unlikely that the average hobbyist will ever have the opportunity to own one, a few words on the Shingleback Skink, *Trachydosaurus rugosus*, are in order. Restricted to Australia,

M. PANZELLA

From New Guinea and adjacent Indonesia, as far west as Sumatra, comes the New Guinea Blue-tongue, *Tiliqua gigas*, the only species that currently is legal to import as wild-caught specimens. It is the only blue-tongue that does not occur in Australia, where all the lizards are protected.

mature in as little as two years, though many will not breed before an age of three years.

As mentioned earlier, these are expensive skinks that are easily sold, and there have been problems with blue-tongue breeding setups being robbed, a rather odd crime at the end of the twentieth century.

where it is common in dry forests and savannahs as well as near-desert conditions, this blackish 12-inch lizard is a close relative of the blue-tongues (it has a bright blue tongue, of course) and has at various times been placed in the genus *Tiliqua* or kept in its own genus. The scales are extremely large and rough

K. H. SWITAK

The living pinecone, a Shingleback, *Trachydosaurus rugosus*, takes a stand against an intruder. These fascinating, gentle, somewhat colonial lizards have been bred in captivity but currently are difficult to find and very expensive.

enough to make the lizard look like a giant pinecone, while the tail is exceedingly short and broad and looks like a second head. Currently Australian laws prohibit its export and captive-bred specimens are virtually unavailable, but Shinglebacks once were fairly common in the hobby.

Their care and natural history are much like the large blue-tongues, requiring a very large terrarium with a hot basking area and cool retreats, broad-spectrum lighting, and a diet of insects along with fruit and the usual vitamin and calcium supplements. Successful breeding seems to require a cooling period with short days like that for the Berber Skink. Females give birth to one or two young about 5 inches long that look like miniatures of the parents. Even young specimens can be sexed with some certainty by the shape of the tail—extremely blunt in females, a bit longer and more pointed in males. Unlike most blue-tongues, Shinglebacks are gentle lizards in captivity and it usually proves possible to leave multiple generations together if the terrarium is large enough. It's a pity these skinks are not more available, because they would make perhaps the best pet skinks of all.

# BASIC BREEDING

If you've read through this entire little book, you will have noted that most skinks are not available captive-bred and few species are bred on a regular basis. For some species the reason for this is simple economics, it being cheaper to import wild-caught specimens than take the time and trouble to breed a lizard that sells for a low price and really is not too spectacular or popular to begin with. Other species simply have resisted the best efforts of commercial and even advanced hobbyist lizard keepers.

It is likely that most skinks from non-extreme environments (i.e., not the deep desert or true rainforest)

W. KASTLE

A mother Pink-tongue, *Tiliqua gerrardi*, with part of her litter.

need a period of cooling and short day lengths to mature the gonads and reach the correct hormonal balance to promote mating. In species from the Northern Hemisphere it has proved possible to over-winter adult skinks much like snake breeders over-winter kingsnakes and rat snakes to promote breeding in the spring. Australian species are more difficult because of the inverted seasons in the Southern Hemisphere, but after a year or

two in captivity in the Northern Hemisphere they often adapt.

Typically, in October the day length is shortened by leaving the lights on for an hour less each week until a day length of only six hours is reached. At the same time food is reduced and the number of hours the basking light is left on are reduced. The main heater (usually an undertank pad) is turned down and then off. By the end of November the terrarium should be dark most of the day and at room temperature. If you can drop the temperature to 60-65°F (16-18°C), so much the better. A water bowl must be supplied, and the lizards must drink at least once a week, even if you have to wake them up for a few minutes. Of course the skinks are not fed during the over-wintering period, and only healthy skinks can be safely kept under these conditions.

About the middle of February (after some eight weeks or more) the process is reversed. The day length is gradually increased back to 12 to 16 hours, the basking area is kept warm longer, and the heater is turned up slowly until normal temperatures are reached. The skinks are given small meals first and then regular feedings as their body temperature is allowed to return to normal. Shortly after the terrarium returns to normal the adults can be placed together if they were kept separately, preferably the male being placed in the female's cage and only one male per cage if you wish to avoid fights.

If this routine does not work, there are several possible explanations. First, the skinks could be too young. Second, females of many skinks probably breed only every two years, and this could be the off year. Third, the adults may not have been sufficiently fed or may be suffering from some bacterial infection or other physical condition making breeding difficult. Try again next year. As a last resort, it might be possible to inspire breeding by suddenly increasing the humidity of the terrarium after a short (a month or so) dry period.

Experimentation could lead to successful breeding of some very interesting skinks that appear only sporadically on the market. Political and environmental regulations already have stopped the regular export of most skinks from Australia, and it is likely that massive deforestation eventually will stop the export of skinks from Indonesia. The constantly expanding Sahara is bound to eventually restrict the availability of skinks from northern Africa, if environmental laws don't stop them first. Political unrest of various types, along with economic problems, in many African countries also may reduce or stop exports. Even trade in wild-caught common five-lined skinks of the southern United States may eventually be regulated out of existence. If you want to ensure the availability of skinks in the future, they will have to be bred in captivity, and every skink enthusiast will have to do his or her part.

Hatching of a pair of *Eumeces laticeps*, Broadhead Skink, eggs. Skink eggs are pretty tough and survive well in almost any typical reptile egg incubator, assuming the female does not actively care for the egg. If the female wants to stay with her eggs, let her—this is safe and saves you a lot of trouble.

R. D. BARTLETT

# SUGGESTED READING

PS-311, 96 pgs, 60+ photos

SK-015, 64 pgs. 40+ photos

PS-316, 128 pgs, 100+ photos

KW-196, 128 pgs, 100+ photos

PS-769, 192 pgs, 120+ photos

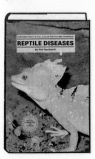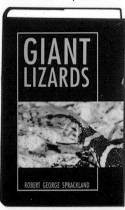

TU-025, 64 pgs, 60+ photos

SK-032, 64 pgs, 40+ photso

YF-111, 32 pgs

TS-145, 288 pgs, 250+ photos

**t.f.h.**

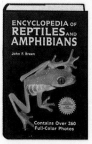

KW-197, 128 pgs, 110+ photos

H-935, 576 pgs, 260+ photos

TS-166, 192 pgs, 170+ photos

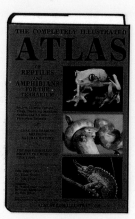

H-1102, 830 pgs, 1800+ Illus and photos

TS-165, 655 pgs, (2 vol.) 1800+ photos